The Meaning
of the Shovel

**The Meaning
of the Shovel**
Martín Espada

STACK
BOOKS

Smokestack Books
PO Box 408, Middlesbrough TS5 6WA
e-mail: info@smokestack-books.co.uk
www.smokestack-books.co.uk

The Meaning of the Shovel

Cover image: *Manuel Molina, Mushroom Worker,*
Kennett Square, Pennsylvania
by Frank Espada.
Copyright 1982 Frank Espada.
Used by permission of the photographer.

Author photograph by Patrick Sylvain.

Printed and bound by Martins the Printers Ltd,
Berwick-upon-Tweed.

Middlesbrough
moving forward

ISBN 978-0-9575747-4-8

Smokestack Books is represented
by Inpress Ltd

for David Velázquez
(1950-2006)

Contents

V. Huelga

VI. Alabanza: In Praise of Local 100

I.
The Meaning
of the Shovel

The Meaning of the Shovel

Barrio René Cisneros, Managua, Nicaragua, June-July 1982

This was the dictator's land
before the revolution.
Now the dictator is exiled to necropolis,
his army brooding in camps on the border,
and the congregation of the landless
stipples the earth with a thousand shacks,
every weather-beaten carpenter
planting a fistful of nails.

Here I dig latrines. I dig because last week
I saw a funeral in the streets of Managua,
the coffin swaddled in a red and black flag,
hoisted by a procession so silent
that even their feet seemed
to leave no sound on the gravel.
He was eighteen, with the border patrol,
when a sharpshooter from the dictator's army
took aim at the back of his head.

I dig because yesterday
I saw four walls of photographs:
the faces of volunteers
in high school uniforms
who taught campesinos to read,
bringing an alphabet
sandwiched in notebooks
to places where the mist never rises
from the trees. All dead,
by malaria or the greedy river
or the dictator's army
swarming the illiterate villages
like a sky full of corn-plundering birds.

I dig because today, in this barrio
without plumbing, I saw a woman
wearing a yellow dress
climb into a barrel of water
to wash herself and the dress
at the same time,
her cupped hands spilling.

I dig because today I stopped digging
to drink an orange soda. In a country
with no glass, the boy kept the treasured bottle
and poured the liquid into a plastic bag
full of ice, then poked a hole with a straw.

I dig because today my shovel
struck a clay bowl centuries old,
the art of ancient fingers
moist with this same earth,
perfect but for one crack in the lip.

I dig because I have hauled garbage
and pumped gas and cut paper
and sold encyclopaedias door to door.
I dig, digging until the passport
in my back pocket saturates with dirt,
because here I work for nothing
and for everything.

Rednecks

Gaithersburg, Maryland

At Scot Gas, Darnestown Road,
the high school boys pumping gas
would snicker at the rednecks.
Every Saturday night there was Earl,
puckering his liquor-smashed face
to announce that he was driving
across the bridge, a bridge spanning
only the whiskey river
that bubbled in his stomach.
Earl's car, one side crumpled like his nose,
would circle slowly around the pumps,
turn signal winking relentlessly.

Another pickup truck morning,
and rednecks. Loitering
in our red uniforms, we watched
as a pickup rumbled through.
We expected: *Fill it with no-lead, boy,
and gimme a cash ticket.*
We expected the farmer with sideburns
and a pompadour.
We, with new diplomas framed
at home, never expected the woman.
Her face was a purple rubber mask
melting off her head, scars rippling down
where the fire seared her freak face,
leaving her a carnival where high school boys
paid a quarter to look, and look away.

No one took the pump. The farmer saw us standing
in our red uniforms, a regiment of illiterate conscripts.
Still watching us, he leaned across the seat of the truck
and kissed her. He kissed her
all over her happy ruined face, kissed her
as I pumped the gas and scraped the windshield
and measured the oil, he kept kissing her.

My Heart Kicked Like a Mouse in a Paper Bag

I was on the cleaning crew for two dollars an hour,
wheeling a trash cart through the aisles at Sears,
panning for cigarettes in the sand of ashtrays, fumbling
fluorescent tubes that exploded when they hit the floor.
I once removed the perfect turd from a urinal, fastidiously
as an Egyptologist handling the scat of a pharaoh.

Some of the janitor's boys were Black men with white hair;
the rest wore badges with missing letters in Spanish.
We heard four bells and galloped across the store.
The janitor sat all day in the boiler room
reading Asian mail-order bride magazines.

I was the boy who swam in trash. I dumped the carts
into the compacter we dubbed the Crusher, then
leaped on the pile to pack it down. Sometimes,
I'd jump on the garbage and burst through
like a skater too heavy for the ice on a frozen lake.
Once a trashman who did not see me pressed the button,
and the walls of the Crusher began to grind. I yelled
and the grinding stopped. The janitor never knew;
he was masturbating in the boiler room.

A stock boy handed me a paper bag one night
as if it were the lunch he forgot to eat, and punched out.
The bag was alive. There was a mouse inside, kicking,
caught sniffing around the Crusher. Bewildered boy
that I was, I called security, department store cops
who loitered at the loading dock, breath hot
from smoking, hunting shoplifters and telling lies
about the war. One of them said: *Where's the mouse?*

When he clapped the bag in his hands it popped, and the pop
made me flinch, and the flinch made him slam the bag again,
till the strawberry stain told me the interrogation was over.
He flipped the bleeding sack at me, and walked away.
My heart kicked like a mouse in a paper bag.

Today I stomp on the trash behind the shed, packing it down for the barrels
I steer into the road. Gathering the cigarettes I do not smoke, that float
in the coffee I do not drink, satisfies the cleaning crew in me.
I hear the four bells, like a fighter with the same headache for forty years.
Sometimes I search the garbage with a flashlight for an unpaid bill,
a bottle of pills, a lost letter, the perfect mouse to liberate.

Do Not Put Dead Monkeys in the Freezer

Monkeys at the laboratory:
monkeys doing countless somersaults
in every cage on the row,
monkeys gobbling Purina Monkey Chow
or Fruit Loops with nervous greedy paws,
monkeys pressing faces
through a grill of steel,
monkeys beating the bars
and showing fang,
monkeys and pink skin
where fur once was,
monkeys with numbers and letters
on bare stomachs,
monkeys clamped and injected, monkeys.

I was a lab coat and rubber gloves
hulking between the cages.
I sprayed down the batter of monkey-shit
coating the bars, fed infant formula in a bottle
to creatures with real fingers,
tested digital thermometers greased
in their asses, and carried boxes of monkeys
to the next experiment.
We gathered the Fear Data, keeping score
as a mechanical head
with blinking red bulbs for eyes
and a siren for a voice
scared monkeys who spun in circles,
chattering instructions
from their bewildered brains.

I did not ask for explanations,
even when I saw the sign
taped to the refrigerator that read:
Do Not Put Dead Monkeys in the Freezer.
I imagined the doctor who ordered the sign,
the moment when the freezer door
swung open on that other face,
and his heart muscle chattered like a monkey.

So I understood
when a monkey leapt from the cage
and bit my thumb through the rubber glove,
leaving a dollop of blood that gleamed
like icing on a cookie.
And I understood when one day, the doctors gone,
a monkey outside the bell curve of the Fear Data
shrieked in revolt, charging
the red-eyed mechanical head
as all the lab coats cheered.

The Bouncer's Confession

I know about the Westerns
where stunt doubles belly-flop
through banisters rigged to collapse
or crash through chairs designed to splinter.
A few times the job was like that.
A bone fragment still floats
in my right ring finger
because the human skull
is harder than any fist.

Mostly, I stood watch at the door
and imagined their skulls
brimming with alcohol
like divers drowning in their own helmets.
Their heads would sag, shaking
to stay awake, elbows sliding out
across the bar.
I gathered their coats. I found their hats.
I rolled up their paper bags
full of sacred objects only I could see.
I interrogated them for an address,
a hometown. I called the cab;
I slung an arm across my shoulders
to walk them down the stairs.

One face still wakes me some mornings.
I remember black-frame eyeglasses
off-balance, his unwashed hair.
I remember the palsy that made claws
of his hands, that twisted his mouth
in the trembling parody of a kiss.
I remember the stack of books he read
beside the beer he would not stop drinking.
I remember his fainted face
pressed against the bar.

This time, I dragged a corkscrewed body
slowly down the stairs, hugged to my ribs,
his books in my other hand,
only to see the impatient taxi
pulling away. I yelled at acceleration smoke,
then fumbled the body with the books
back up the stairs, and called the cab again.

No movie barrooms. No tall stranger
shot the body spread-eagled across the broken table.
No hero, with a hero's uppercut, knocked them out,
not even me. I carried them out.

The Rifle in My Hands

Four dollar an hour bouncer:
another grunting shove
and blast of obscenities,
cheekbone scraped numb,
heart squeezed again
with the narcotic of the fight,
I heard the rifle crack of my fist
against a beer-dizzy skull;

but listening
for the first time
to that rifle in my hands,
I became a soldier on strike,
weapons dropped amid the bullets' sleet,
hands sick and trembling, face pelted
in the flailing storm of the brawl.

Knuckles dark blue lumps
by morning, I quit the bar
and hid my purple heart
in white bandages.

Transient Hotel Sky at the Hour of Sleep

On the late shift, front desk,
midnight to 8 AM,
we watched the sky through crusted windows,
till the clouds swirled away
like water in the drain
of a steel sink.

In the clouded liquid light
human shapes would harden,
an Army jacket staggering
against the banister at bar-time,
a coal-skinned man
drifting through the lobby
moaning to himself
about Mississippi,
a known arsonist
squeezing his head
into the microwave oven
with a giggle.

As we studied the white face
of the clock above the desk,
fluorescent hum of 4 AM,
a cowboy bragged
about buying good boots
for 19 cents from a retarded man,
then swaggered out the door
with a pickaxe
and a treasure map.
The janitor mopped the floor
nostalgic for Vietnam snapshots
confiscated at the airport,
peasant corpses with jaws
lopsided in a song of missing teeth.

Slowly the sky was a comfort,
like the pillow of a patient
sick for decades
and sleeping at last.
At the hour of sleep
a man called Johnson
trotted down the hallway
and leaned out the window,
then again, haunting
the fifth floor
in a staring litany
of gestures, so even
the security guard on rounds
wrote in the logbook for social workers
who never kept a schedule at night.
Johnson leaped
through the greasy pane of sky
at 5 AM,
refused suicide in flight,
and kicking struggled to stand in the air,
but snapped his ankles on the sidewalk
and burst his head on the curb,
scalp flapped open like the lid
on a bucket of red paint.

The newspaper shocked mouths
that day, but the transient hotel sky
drained pale as usual,
and someone pissed in the ashtray
by the desk, then leered
at the jabbering smokers.

A Travelling Salesman in the Gardens of Paradise

for Gisela

Jardines del Paraíso: The Gardens of Paradise,
or so we'd say, staring into our coffee, whenever
we translated the name of the public housing projects
where my grandmother smoked on the porch,
watching the trade in dollars and drugs
swiftly move from hand to hand
in Río Piedras, Puerto Rico.

One night a visitor called her name
through the shutters of the window,
going door to door with something to sell:
a car battery in his hands, offered with the pride
of a diver showing off a treasure chest
salvaged from the bottom of the sea.

He was a travelling salesman in the Gardens of Paradise.
I was a travelling salesman once, selling encyclopaedias
door to door, buying only the cheapest leads
from people who wrote: *I want to win a free encyclopaedia.*
Don't send me a salesman. Door after door slapped shut.
I quit one day, when the cops spotted me reading maps
spread across the steering wheel and held me for hours
in the parking lot, suspected of stealing my own car.
The little cop wore sunglasses in the rain, asking repeatedly
if I was wanted by the police. *I don't know,* I said. *Do you want me?*

Let him in, I proclaimed that night in the Gardens of Paradise.
We broke the reverie of arroz con pollo steaming on the fork.
Cousin Gisela greeted the salesman with his offering,
then had a vision pure and brilliant as the halo of Jesus on the wall:
her car in the parking lot with the hood propped up
and the battery missing. *Did you get that from my car?*
asked Gisela, like a teacher aggravated by another theft
of cookies from her desk. *You put that back right now.*
With apologies and a bow, he did.

He was a tecato, Gisela said, another junkie with a face
from the neighbourhood. The next day my grandmother,
who believed that even junkies have a place in Paradise,
called to the same tecato through the window,
handed him her last five dollars,
and sent him to the store for cigarettes.

There would be buying and selling
that night in the Gardens of Paradise,
and witnesses who would never testify
chain-smoking on the porch.

II.
The Legal Aid
Lawyer Has
An Epiphany

Who Burns for the Perfection of Paper

At sixteen, I worked after high school hours
at a printing plant
that manufactured legal pads:
Yellow paper stacked seven feet high
and leaning
as I slipped cardboard
between the pages,
then brushed red glue
up and down the stack.
No gloves: fingertips required
for the perfection of paper,
smoothing the exact rectangle.
Sluggish by 9 PM, the hands
would slide along suddenly sharp paper,
and gather slits thinner than the crevices
of the skin, hidden.
Then the glue would sting,
hands oozing
till both palms burned
at the punch clock.

Ten years later, in law school,
I knew that every legal pad
was glued with the sting of hidden cuts,
that every open lawbook
was a pair of hands
upturned and burning.

City of Coughing and Dead Radiators

Chelsea, Massachusetts

I cannot evict them
from my insomniac nights,
tenants in the city of coughing
and dead radiators.
They bang the radiators
like cold hollow marimbas;
they cry out
to unseen creatures
skittering across their feet
in darkness;
they fold hands over plates
to protect food
from ceilings black with roaches.

And they answer the call
of the list,
all evictions in court,
brays the clerk.
Quiet and dutiful
as spectral troops returning,
they file into the courtroom,
crowding the gallery:
the patient one from El Salvador,
shoemakers' union refugee,
slapping his neck
to show where that vampire
of an army bullet
pierced his uncle's windpipe;
the red-haired woman
with no electricity
but for the drug's heat
swimming in the pools
of her blue bruises,

white-skinned as the candles
she lives by,
who will move this afternoon
for a hundred dollars;
the prostitute swollen
with pregnancy and sobbing
as the landlady
sneers *miscarriage*
before a judge
poking his broken hearing aid;
the girl surrounded by a pleading carousel
of children, in Spanish bewilderment,
sleepless and rat-vigilant,
who wins reluctant extermination
but loses the youngest,
lead paint-retarded;
the man alcohol-puffed,
graph of scars
stretching across his belly,
locked out, shirt stolen,
arrested at the hearing
for the rampage
of his detox hallucinations;
the Guatemalan boy, who listens
through the wall
for his father's landlord-defiant staccato,
jolted awake
by flashes of the landlord
floating over the bed,
parade balloon
waving a kitchen knife.

For all those sprawled down stairs
with the work boot's crusted map
printed on the back,
the creases of the judge's face
collapse into a fist.
As we shut files
and click briefcases
to leave,
a loud-faced man
trumpets from the gallery:
Death to Legal Aid.

Mi Vida: Wings of Fright

Chelsea, Massachusetts, 1987

The refugee's run
across the desert borderlands
carved wings of fright
into his forehead,
growing more crooked
with every eviction notice
in this waterfront city of the north.

He sat in the office for the poor,
daughter burrowed asleep
on one shoulder,
and spoke to the lawyer
with a voice trained obedient
in the darkness of church confessionals
and police barracks, Guatemalan dusk.

The lawyer nodded through papers,
glancing up only when the girl awoke
to spout white vomit on the floor
and her father's shirt.
Mi vida: My life, he said,
then said again, as he bundled her
to the toilet.

This was how the lawyer,
who, like the fortune-teller,
had a bookshelf of prophecy
but a cabinet empty of cures,
found himself
kneeling on the floor
with a paper towel.

The Broken Window of Rosa Ramos

Chelsea, Massachusetts, 1991

Rosa Ramos could spread her palm
at the faucet for hours
without cold water
ever hissing hot,
while the mice darted
like runaway convicts
from a hole in the kitchen floor.

The landlord was a spy,
clicking his key in the door unheard
to haunt the living room,
peeking for the thrill of young skin,
a pasty dead-faced man still hungry.

Her husband was dead.
She knew this
from *El Vocero* newspaper,
the picture of his grinning face
sprayed with the black sauce of blood,
a bullet-feast.
Rosa shows his driver's license,
a widow's identification,
with the laminated plastic
cracking across his eyes,
so that he watches her
through a broken window.

She leaves the office
rehearsing with the lawyer
new words in English
for the landlord:
Get out. Get out. Get out.

Thieves of Light

Chelsea, Massachusetts, 1991

We all knew about Gus:
the locksmith, the Edison man, and me.
We heard about the welfare hotel,
where he stacked clothes
on the sidewalk for the garbage truck
if no rent was paid by Wednesday morning.
We heard about the triple deckers,
where he heaved
someone else's chair or television
from the third floor, and raged
like a drunk blaming his woman
till the pleading tenant agreed to leave.
There was word he even shot a cop
twenty years ago, but the jury
knew Gus too, studying cuticles
or the courtroom clock
as the foreman said not guilty.
The only constable in Chelsea
wore his gun in a shoulder holster,
drooped his cigarette at a dangerous angle,
yet claimed that Gus
could not be found on Broadway
to serve a summons in his hand.

This is how we knew Gus:
Luisa saw the sludge plop
from the faucet, the mice
dropping from the ceiling,
shook her head and said no rent,
still said no after his fist
buckled the bolted door.
In the basement, Gus hit switches.
The electric arteries in the walls

stopped pumping, stove cold,
heat off, light bulbs gray.
She lived three months in darkness,
the wax from her candle spreading
over the kitchen table like a calendar
of the constant night,
sleeping in her coat, a beggar
in the underworld kingdom of rodents.
When Luisa came to me, a lawyer
who knew Spanish,
she kept coughing
into her fist, apologizing
with every cough.

So three strangers
gathered in the hallway.
The locksmith
kneeled before the knob
on the basement door,
because I asked him
to be a burglar today.
The Edison man swallowed dryly,
because I asked him
to smuggle electricity today,
forget Gus's promise
of crushed fingers.
And me: the lawyer, tightly
rolling a court order in my hand
like a newspaper to swing at flies,
so far from the leather-bound books
of law school, the treatises
on the constitution
of some other country.

We worked quickly, thieves of light.
The door popped open,
as in a dream of welcome,
swaying with the locksmith's fingers.

The Edison man pressed his palms
against the fuse boxes
and awakened the sleeping wires
in the walls. I kept watch by the door,
then crept upstairs, past Gus's office
where shadows and voices
drove the blood in my wrist
still faster. I tapped on Luisa's door.
I had to see if the light was on.

She stared at me
as if the rosary
had brought me here
with this sudden glow from the ceiling,
a stove where rice and beans
could simmer, sleep without a coat.
I know there were no angels
swimming in that dim yellow globe,
but there was a light louder than Gus,
so much light
I had to close my eyes.

Offerings to an Ulcerated God

Chelsea, Massachusetts

Mrs. López refuses to pay rent,
and we want her out,
the landlord's lawyer said,
tugging at his law school ring.
The judge called for an interpreter,
but all the interpreters were gone,
trafficking in Spanish
at the criminal session
on the second floor.

A volunteer stood up in the gallery.
Mrs. López showed the interpreter
a poker hand of snapshots,
the rat curled in a glue trap
next to the refrigerator,
the water frozen in the toilet,
a door without a doorknob
(No rent for this. I know the law
and I want to speak,
she whispered to the interpreter).

Tell her she has to pay
and she has ten days to get out,
the judge commanded, rose
so the rest of the courtroom rose,
and left the bench. Suddenly
the courtroom clattered
with the end of business:
the clerk of the court
gathered her files
and the bailiff went to lunch.

Mrs. López stood before the bench,
still holding up her fan of snapshots
like an offering this ulcerated god
refused to taste,
while the interpreter
felt the burning
bubble in his throat
as he slowly turned to face her.

The Legal Aid Lawyer has an Epiphany

Chelsea, Massachusetts

When I bounced off the bus for work
at Legal Aid this morning,
I found the spiky halo of a hole
in the front window of the office,
as if some drunk had rammed
the thorn-crowned head of Jesus
through the glass.
I say *Jesus* because I followed
the red handprints on the brick
and there he was next door,
a bust in the window
of the botánica,
blood in his hair,
his eyes a bewildered blue
cast heavenward, hoping
for an airlift away from here.
The sign on the door
offered a manicure
with every palm reading.

The Secret of the Legal Secretary's Cigarette Smoke

for my mother

Cubicled women
peck at computers,
observed by the senior partner,
bowed and vigilant
as a gray monk,
watch in hand
at exactly 9 A.M.

Genuflection
to ashen priests of commerce:
bodies gliding in a hush
across the carpet
leave coffee and pastries
for aristocratic hands
to contemplate.

At break time,
the senior partner's name
is a spat breath of cigarette smoke,
and even the quiet
religious woman
sneers.

III.
My Native
Costume

My Native Costume

When you come to visit,
said a teacher
from the suburban school,
don't forget to wear
your native costume.

But I'm a lawyer,
I said.
My native costume
is a pinstriped suit.

You know, the teacher said,
a Puerto Rican costume.

Like a guayabera? The shirt? I said.
But it's February.

The children want to see
a native costume,
the teacher said.

So I went
to the suburban school,
embroidered guayabera
short-sleeved shirt
over a turtleneck,
and said, *Look kids,*
cultural adaptation.

The Poet's Son Watches his Father Leave for Another Gig

Once again
you're choosing
between dignity
and Christmas

Inheritance of Waterfalls and Sharks

for my son Klemente

In 1898, with the infantry from Illinois,
the boy who would become the poet Sandburg
rowed his captain's Saint Bernard ashore
at Guánica, and watched as the captain
lobbed cubes of steak at the canine snout.
The troops speared mangos with bayonets
like many suns thudding with shredded yellow flesh
to earth. General Miles, who chained Geronimo
for the photograph in sepia of the last renegade,
promised Puerto Rico the *blessings of enlightened civilization.*
Private Sandburg marched, peeking at a book
nested in his palm for the words of Shakespeare.

Dazed in blue wool and sunstroke, they stumbled up the mountain
to Utuado, learned the war was over, and stumbled away.
Sandburg never met great-great-grand uncle Don Luis,
who wore a linen suit that would not wrinkle,
read with baritone clarity scenes from Hamlet
house to house for meals of rice and beans,
the Danish prince and his soliloquy– *ser o no ser* –
saluted by rum, the ghost of Hamlet's father wandering
through the ceremonial ball-courts of the Taíno.

In Caguas or Cayey Don Luis
was the reader at the cigar factory,
newspapers in the morning,
Cervantes or Marx in the afternoon,
rocking with the whirl of an unseen sword
when Quijote roared his challenge to giants,
weaving the tendrils of his beard when he spoke
of labour and capital, as the tabaqueros
rolled leaves of tobacco to smolder in distant mouths.

Maybe he was the man of the same name
who published a sonnet in the magazine of browning leaves
from the year of the Great War and the cigar strike.
He disappeared; there were rumours of Brazil,
inciting cane-cutters or marrying the patrón's daughter,
maybe both, but always the reader, whipping Quijote's sword overhead.

Another century, and still the warships scavenge
Puerto Rico's beaches with wet snouts. For practice,
Navy guns hail shells coated with uranium over Vieques
like a boy spinning his first curveball;
to the fisherman on the shore, the lung is a net
and the tumor is a creature with his own face, gasping.

This family has no will, no house, no farm, no island.
But today the great-great-great-grand nephew of Don Luis,
not yet ten, named for a jailed poet and fathered by another poet,
in a church of the Puritan colony called Massachusetts,
wobbles on a crate and grabs the podium
to read his poem about El Yunque waterfalls
and Achill basking sharks, and shouts:
I love this.

Hard-Handed Men of Athens

Theseus: What are they that do play it?
Philostrate: Hard-handed men, that work in Athens here,
Which never labour'd in their minds till now.

A Midsummer Night's Dream, Act V, Scene I

We are the hard-handed men of Athens, the rude Mechanicals:
the tailor, the weaver, the tinker, the bellows-mender.
Tonight we are actors in the forest, off the grid, surrounded
in the dark by fairies and spirits, snakes and coyotes.
Carnivorous vegans live in these woods. They leave the drum circle
to nibble at the sliced ham I smuggle in the folds of my costume.

I am three hundred pounds. The director of the company
saw me and said: 'You are the Wall.' Two weeks ago I fell
off a wall, stepping into the darkness like a cartoon character
walking on air, waving *bye-bye.* I belly-flopped in a puddle of mud.
An elderly bystander, as if on cue, spoke her only line: 'Are you OK?'
I am not OK. I have a fractured elbow. I wear a sling under my Wall costume,
the Styrofoam bricks and plastic vines, the wooden beam across my shoulders.
I cannot remember my lines. I hide the script in my sling with the ham.

The play begins. No one can find Lysander. He is in the bathroom
with dysentery. Theseus improvises dialogue in iambic pentameter.
His voice echoes and scares the coyotes in the hills. They howl
back at him. A snake writes his name in the dirt by my feet.
I tell no one. I don't want the fairies to panic. Cobweb and Mustardseed
might run into the Tiki torches, and then their fairy wings would explode,
and the nearest hospital is forty miles away. The Tiki torches
are the only source of light off the grid. It's Shakespeare in the Dark.
The woman playing Peter Quince is mean to small children.
When Bottom turns into a donkey and the Mechanicals flee,
I stand behind her and let her bounce off my chest. She falls down.
I want her to fall down. I ask: 'Are you OK?' She is not OK. Fairy Queen
Titania's bed sways in the trees, threatening to topple and kill us all.

At the wedding of Theseus, Duke of Athens, we play Pyramus and Thisbe.
The aristocrats laugh at us, real actors on loan from the highbrow
Shakespearean company in the valley, and we snarl back at them.
I am the Wall. I am inspired. I lift Pyramus and Thisbe into the air
and slam them together for their kiss. The beam across my shoulders
cracks. The crack alarms the carnivorous vegans on picnic blankets
watching the show. Some think the crack is my leg breaking. Some think
the crack is a gunshot. Suddenly it's Ford's Theatre and I'm Lincoln.
Or maybe I'm John Wilkes Booth. The jagged beam presses into my neck,
against the artery in my neck, like the fangs of a vampire hungry for ham.
One stumble and *A Midsummer Night's Dream* ends in a bloodbath.

I bellow my last line: 'Thus Wall away doth go.' I do a soft-shoe offstage.
Five people pull the Wall costume over my head. Somebody asks: 'Are you OK?'
I am not OK. Then I see my son onstage. He is twelve. He is Moonshine.
He cradles a half-blind Chihuahua and says, 'This dog, my dog.'
He lifts his lantern high, and his lantern is the moon. Even the sneering
Hippolyta, Queen of the Amazons, must admit: 'Well shone, Moon.'
This moon shines like an uncirculated Kennedy half-dollar from the days
when Kennedy was a martyred saint. The coyotes do not howl.
The crickets fall silent. Even the fairies cease their gossip and giggling.
We are the hard-handed men of Athens. This dog is our dog.

The Man in the Duck Suit

for Todd Godwin (1957-2011)

He wore a duck suit for my Super 8 movie,
back in the days when I wanted to make movies,
before I found out that I couldn't buy
cameras or film with food stamps. I borrowed
a camera and a shotgun, then rented a duck costume
for the star of my crime thriller, *In Cold Duck*.

In between takes, he would pull the duck's head off
and tuck it underneath his arm, half-human, half-waterfowl,
curly beard and bright yellow feathers, a creature from the mythology
of ancient Assyria pontificating in a New Jersey British accent
about the art of improvisation. After the last take,
he wandered out onto my porch in full duck regalia,
waving the shotgun at passing cars on Johnson Street.

Thirty years later, the hunters of Wisconsin still shiver in the reeds
as they recall the Monster Duck who hunted humans. I know
he was only a man in a duck suit, a secret I can now reveal.
He was my Bigfoot, glimpsed on grainy film, the camera shaking.

The Death of Carmen Miranda

Dying on television,
on *The Jimmy Durante Show,*
spinning another samba for the tourists,
she staggered beneath the banana headdress
and dropped to one knee.
The audience began to giggle
at the wobbly pyramid of bananas,
but the comedian with the fat nose and the fedora
growled *Stop the music!* and lifted her up.
I cannot find my breath, Carmen said,
fingers fanning across her chest.
The mouth of the camera opened
to chuckle at her accent, but then
widened into an astonished *Oh.*

Later that night, at the mansion,
her maid found Carmen sleeping without breath,
could not unlock the mirror from her fingers.
The hair no one saw on television was unpinned,
grown long beneath the banana headdress,
bleached yellow like the bananas.

Latin Night at the Pawnshop

Chelsea, Massachusetts, Christmas, 1987

The apparition of a salsa band
gleaming in the Liberty Loan
pawnshop window:

Golden trumpet,
silver trombone,
congas, maracas, tambourine,
all with price tags dangling
like the city morgue ticket
on a dead man's toe.

IV.
The Toolmaker
Unemployed

The Saint Vincent de Paul Food Pantry Stomp

Madison, Wisconsin, 1980

Waiting for the carton of food
given with Christian suspicion
even to agency-certified charity cases
like me,
thin and brittle
as uncooked linguini,
anticipating the factory-damaged cans
of tomato soup, beets, three-bean salad
in a welfare cornucopia,
I spotted a squashed dollar bill
on the floor, and with
a Saint Vincent de Paul food pantry stomp
pinned it under my sneaker,
tied my laces meticulously,
and stuffed the bill in my sock
like a smuggler of diamonds,
all beneath the plaster statue wingspan
of Saint Vinnie,
who was unaware
of the dance
named in his honour
by a maraca player
in the salsa band
of the unemployed.

Watch Me Swing

I was the fifth man hired
for the city welfare cleaning crew
at the old Paterson Street ballpark,
Class A minor leagues.
Opening Day was over,
and we raked the wooden benches
for the droppings of the crowd:
wrappers, spilled cups, scorecards,
popcorn cartons, chewed and spat hot dogs,
a whiskey bottle, a condom dried on newspaper.

We swung our brooms,
pausing to watch home runs sail
through April imagination
over the stone fence three hundred feet away,
baseball cracking off the paint factory sign
across Washington Street.
We shuffled and kicked,
plowed and pushed
through the clinging garbage,
savoring our minimum wages.

When the sweeping was done,
and the grandstand benches
clean as Sunday morning pews,
the team business manager
inspected the aisles,
reviewed the cleaning crew
standing like broomstick cadets
and said:
We only need four.
I was the fifth man hired.

As the business manager
strode across the outfield
back to his office,
I wanted to leap the railing,
crouch at home plate
and swing my broom,
aiming a smacked baseball
for the back of his head,
yelling *watch me swing, boss,*
watch me swing.

The Foreman's Wallet

At the printing plant,
I operated the machine
that shrink-wrapped paper
in clear plastic.
The bosses were Jehovah's Witnesses,
men pale as cheese
who sold Bibles door to door
on Sundays. They were polite,
and assembled the crew one night
to explain politely
that all of us were unemployed
by 11 PM:
No government contracts.
The plywood office door
clicked shut.

No one knows who set the first
wheel of paper rolling across the floor,
who speared the soda machine
with a two-by-four,
who winged unstapled copies of Commander's Digest
so they flew, with their diagrams of bombers,
through the room. Towers of legal pads collapsed,
fist-fired paper grenades hissed overhead.
A forklift truck without a driver bumped blindly
down the aisle, and we all saluted.
If we knew any songs, we would have sung them.

Saboteurs were unscrewing the punch-clock
and rearranging the parts like palaeontologists
toying with the backbone of a stegosaurus
when the foreman arrived,
his adolescent voice whining authority.
He was my last job.

The conspiracy to shrink-wrap
the foreman's head, turning red
in a wrestling hold, was a failure.
His skull was too big
to squeeze through the machine,
and even the radicals among us relented
when his eyes steamed with tears.
So we shrink-wrapped the foreman's wallet,
gleaming in the fresh plastic
like half a pound of hamburger.

'Here's your wallet,' I said. And mine.

The Chair in the Dragon's Mouth

Chelsea, Massachusetts

Once I worked in the kitchen at Ned's,
where every day I flattened
the dough of a hundred pizzas
refrigerated for weeks.
I scooped limp spaghetti
floating in a vat of ice water
and heated it under a faucet.
I was ordered to wash the walls
with dish detergent
for the Board of Health inspection.
I had a jukebox headache.

Fifteen years later, in Chelsea,
I stood below a rainstorm, blinking
at a drainpipe that gushed helplessly.
The 111 bus was stalled
by flooding like pneumonia in the sewer's lungs,
so I hid under my coat and ran
into Mystic River House of Pizza.
I remember nothing about the woman
behind the counter
except a blonde ponytail
and the glass of water she gave me
because I had no money.
Her husband rinsed dishes in the sink.
Together we waited till the green awning
of the pizza shop stopped dripping.

I returned on another day
when the buses could not pass.
Dropped off a block away,
I winced at kitchen smoke,
then saw the yellow warning tape
gift-wrapping the street.
I stood before Mystic River House of Pizza:
the burst ceiling dangling
its entrails, a chair upside down
through the window of jagged glass
jutting like teeth in a dragon's mouth.
The neighbours talked about
a greasy rag in flames, tossed
from the grill to the sink,
the fire jumping nimbly
to the garbage can, a hazy glow
blackening the room.
Later, I found a menu
from the pizza shop
folded in my coat.

The wrecking ball
pounded down half the buildings
on the block. There was rubble,
then earth, then the first grass,
rumours of a parking lot.
With the new seasons,
the neighbours stopped repeating
her words, what she said
to the weary fire-fighters about her husband:
Please don't tell him how it happened.
Please don't tell him it was me.

The Toolmaker Unemployed

Connecticut River Valley, 1992

The toolmaker
is sixty years old,
unemployed
since the letter
from his boss
at the machine shop.

He carries
a cooler of soda
everywhere,
so as not to carry
a flask of whiskey.

During the hours
of his shift,
he is building a barn
with borrowed lumber
or hacking at trees
in the yard.

The family watches
and listens to talk
of a bullet
in the forehead,
maybe for himself,
maybe for the man
holding the second mortgage.

Sometimes
he stares down
into his wallet.

V.
Huelga

Federico's Ghost

The story is
that whole families of fruit-pickers
still crept between the furrows
of the field at dusk,
when for reasons of whiskey or whatever
the crop-duster plane sprayed anyway,
floating a pesticide drizzle
over the pickers
who thrashed like dark birds
in a glistening white net,
except for Federico,
a skinny boy who stood apart
in his own green row,
and, knowing the pilot
would not understand in Spanish
that he was the son of a whore,
instead jerked his arm
and thrust an obscene finger.

The pilot understood.
He circled the plane and sprayed again,
watching a fine gauze of poison
drift over the brown bodies
that cowered and scurried on the ground,
and aiming for Federico,
leaving the skin beneath his shirt
wet and blistered,
but still pumping his finger at the sky.

After Federico died,
rumours at the labour camp
told of tomatoes picked and smashed at night,
growers muttering of vandal children
or communists in camp,
first threatening to call Immigration,
then promising every Sunday off
if only the smashing of tomatoes would stop.

Still tomatoes were picked and squashed
in the dark,
and the old women in camp
said it was Federico,
labouring after sundown
to cool the burns on his arms,
flinging tomatoes
at the crop-duster
that hummed like a mosquito
lost in his ear,
and kept his soul awake.

The Florida Citrus Growers Association Responds to a Proposed Law Requiring Hand-Washing Facilities in the Fields

An orange,
squeezed on the hands,
is an adequate substitute
for soap and water

Leo Blue's and the Tiger Rose

Mitchell walked three miles
for cigarettes
and a telephone call to Legal Aid:
Take me away from Leo Blue's, he said.

Labour camp: tin shacks and a sand pit,
gathering place for apparitions
killed by the heat;
through the tin surface and screens
the sun crawls like a bright spider
that startles the eyes and heart,
a sweat-demon slowly walking.

This is a row of dark-skinned men
with old shoes,
recruited from the mission shelter
in Tampa, drink-poisoned then,
still blurred;
a swallow of Tiger Rose wine
before cucumber picking
in the swollen light of morning.
They dump cucumber buckets
for another swallow
of the craved wine
from a crew-leader's truck.

All day bending
like something storm-broken
and left to sway,
dream scarecrows
with stiff hands picking.
Ten hours gone.

Return to camp,
back to the crew-leader's gospel music tapes
loudly preaching,
minimum wage signs no one can read
posted in the kitchen,
camp meals of pigs' ears and pinto beans
deducted with brown pay-envelope arithmetic:
Mitchell works three days
for six dollars.
We wait
as he soaps the farmer's car
to pay for the last
of his meals.

We leave the brilliance of sharp-angled roof,
old shoes unclaimed
near hunchback-mattress.

Julio Signing His Name

Julio cheats
signing his name,
copying slowly
from his Social Security card,
man's hand
scratching letters child-crooked.

But Julio's black hand
was schooled for lettuce-picking,
not lawsuits.

The Drought

for Rosa Escamilla, Lubbock, Texas

Rosa's body stopped growing at the age of twelve.
Ten hours a day she would labour in the cotton fields,
sun spiking her eyelids, bent beside her father
and the years dying in the drought of his hands.

Soon the jug was empty, and the muscles
scraping in her throat would tell her: *water.*
Twelve years old, Rosa studied the road
and imagined a man driving a silver car
that meandered through the cotton fields
to bring her water, chilled in a long
bright glass, close enough to see
the moisture-beads evaporate.

Twenty years after her body stopped growing,
Rosa hides a peasant daughter's hallucination
in her eyelids, a silver car snaking through the fields,
the first drops for the drought cracking her lips.

The Right Hand of a Mexican Farmworker in Somerset County, Maryland

A rosary tattoo
between thumb
and forefinger
means that
every handful
of crops and dirt
is a prayer,
means that Christ
had hard hands
too

Huelga

for César Chávez, 1927-1993

Because of that brown face,
smooth weather-beaten soil;
because of these eyes,
ringed by rain-hungry creek beds;
because of those peasant fingers
curling around a shovel so it became
a picket sign or a flag flying the black eagle of union;
because of that voice, speaking the word *boycott*
like a benediction, the word *huelga*
as if the name of a god with calluses:

The red in the wine stings our eyes
with its brightness,
the grape is a circle more like the world
and less like a silver dollar.

VI.
Alabanza:
in Praise of
Local 100

Jorge the Church Janitor Finally Quits

Cambridge, Massachusetts, 1989

No one asks
where I am from,
I must be
from the country of janitors,
I have always mopped this floor.
Honduras, you are a squatter's camp
outside the city
of their understanding.

No one can speak
my name,
I host the fiesta
of the bathroom,
stirring the toilet
like a punchbowl.
The Spanish music of my name
is lost
when the guests complain
about toilet paper.

What they say
must be true:
I am smart,
but I have a bad attitude.

No one knows
that I quit tonight,
maybe the mop
will push on without me,
sniffing along the floor
like a crazy squid
with stringy gray tentacles.
They will call it Jorge.

The Janitor's Garden

for Félix Rodríguez, Aibonito, Puerto Rico 1997

The office building at forty-second and Lexington
sat awaiting the night janitor
like an executive anticipating a shoeshine:
sixty floors mopped and waxed every night,
five nights a week, fifty weeks a year,
for forty-five years: 675,000 floors gleaming.
The ammonia streamed its clear poison
in a cascade, as if from the temple of Ammon
in faraway Egypt, where ammonia began.

He inhaled the burning breath of ammonia
for half a century, and did not die.
He polished the floors for the polished shoes
of industrialists while they slept,
yet did not sleep with rum or wake in sweat.
He stacked the toilet paper of lawyers after midnight
as they stacked contracts and wills,
and did not quiver with desire for their paper.
The janitor kept his garden every night.

When the elevator doors opened
and his mop slid across the floor,
on that glistening spot an orange tree
would sprout, roots fingering through the tile.
A swipe of the mop
and another orange tree scraped the ceiling
with its unfolding fan of branches,
then again till the hallway
was an orange grove in bloom, brilliant
with the trees of China, as we say in Puerto Rico.

The scent of oranges banished ammonia,
and the cleaning crew dripped pulp and juice
to their elbows. Not one sneezed or coughed
in Manhattan slush, walking home after night shift.

On some mornings, a secretary would report
that the floors had been waxed with orange juice,
an errand boy might find peels floating
in all the toilets, or the day janitor discover
an orange in a paper bag scrawled with his name.
The lawyers snorted, blamed the menstrual cycle
or the imagination of coloured people, then went to lunch.

Today Félix keeps his garden
in the hills of Aibonito. He is bald as an orange.
Without the ceiling pressing down
the trees become celestial jugglers
levitating orange planets. I climb to the roof
and soak my beard with luminous fruit
as he glances up from the garden,
leaning on his mop.

Prayer for Brother Burglar

for David Velázquez (1950-2006)

He was once the adolescent,
green eyes alert, who could ease
locked bedroom doors aside
to scoop jewelry, cameras, clock radios,
awakening no one.

The years grew swirls on his knuckles
and red flags in the hollows of his hands.
A bullhorn man among strikers,
driving for the Union Cab Company,
he called himself *a taxista Marxista-Leninista*
and told of marching through his history
with the limbs of a dead street rebel
spread-eagled across shoulders,
rifles shaken overhead,
the blackout that follows the billy club,
each compañero and each cop named
with the witness of a hand
missing one thumb.

Once he clicked off the meter
and tickled my door open
to prove his weather-brown hands still clever
even missing one thumb,
work boots stamping mud through the room
like tire tracks on the sidewalk,
a hard-bellied man in overalls and baseball cap
booming *The Internationale* at me
on the toilet.

Many jobs later, he was fired for words
drilled in the face
of an embezzling boss, and this
after spending his cash
on a racehorse
too old for anyone else to buy.
He draped his heavy horse blankets
on a clothesline in my apartment for two weeks,
then bounced away in a rattling white van.

May his hands still be smart;
may his thumb grow back
to better grip the bullhorn
or the boss's collar.

The Mexican Cabdriver's Poem for his Wife, Who has Left Him

We were sitting in traffic
on the Brooklyn Bridge,
so I asked the poets
in the back seat of my cab
to write a poem for you.

They asked
if you are like the moon
or the trees.

I said no,
she is like the bridge
when there is so much traffic
I have time
to watch the boats
on the river.

For the Jim Crow Mexican Restaurant in Cambridge, Massachusetts, where my Cousin Esteban was Forbidden to Wait Tables Because he Wears Dreadlocks

I have noticed that the hostess in peasant dress,
the wait staff and the boss
share the complexion of a flour tortilla.
I have spooked the servers at my table
by trilling the word *burrito*.
I am aware of your T-shirt solidarity
with the refugees of the Américas,
since they steam in your kitchen.
I know my cousin Esteban the sculptor
rolled tortillas in your kitchen with the fingertips
of ancestral Puerto Rican cigar makers.
I understand he wanted to be a waiter,
but you proclaimed his black dreadlocks unclean,
so he hissed in Spanish
and his apron collapsed on the floor.

May La Migra handcuff the wait staff
as suspected illegal aliens from Canada;
may a hundred mice dive from the oven
like diminutive leaping dolphins
during your Board of Health inspection;
may the kitchen workers strike, sitting
with folded hands as enchiladas blacken
and twisters of smoke panic the customers;
may a Zapatista squadron commandeer the refrigerator,
liberating a pillar of tortillas at gunpoint;
may you hallucinate dreadlocks
braided in thick vines around your ankles;
and may the Aztec gods pinned like butterflies
to the menu wait for you in the parking lot
at midnight, demanding that you spell their names.

Alabanza: In Praise of Local 100

*for the 43 members of Hotel Employees and Restaurant Employees
Local 100, working at the Windows on the World restaurant, who
lost their lives in the attack on the World Trade Centre*

Alabanza. Praise the cook with a shaven head
and a tattoo on his shoulder that said *Oye,*
a blue-eyed Puerto Rican with people from Fajardo,
the harbour of pirates centuries ago.
Praise the lighthouse in Fajardo, candle
glimmering white to worship the dark saint of the sea.
Alabanza. Praise the cook's yellow Pirates cap
worn in the name of Roberto Clemente, his plane
that flamed into the ocean loaded with cans for Nicaragua,
for all the mouths chewing the ash of earthquakes.
Alabanza. Praise the kitchen radio, dial clicked
even before the dial on the oven, so that music and Spanish
rose before bread. Praise the bread. *Alabanza.*

Praise Manhattan from a hundred and seven flights up,
like Atlantis glimpsed through the windows of an ancient aquarium.
Praise the great windows where immigrants from the kitchen
could squint and almost see their world, hear the chant of nations:
Ecuador, México, República Dominicana,
Haiti, Yemen, Ghana, Bangladesh.
Alabanza. Praise the kitchen in the morning,
where the gas burned blue on every stove
and exhaust fans fired their diminutive propellers,
hands cracked eggs with quick thumbs
or sliced open cartons to build an altar of cans.
Alabanza. Praise the busboy's music, the *chime-chime*
of his dishes and silverware in the tub.
Alabanza. Praise the dish-dog, the dishwasher
who worked that morning because another dishwasher
could not stop coughing, or because he needed overtime
to pile the sacks of rice and beans for a family

floating away on some Caribbean island plagued by frogs.
Alabanza. Praise the waitress who heard the radio in the kitchen
and sang to herself about a man gone. *Alabanza.*

After the thunder wilder than thunder,
after the shudder deep in the glass of the great windows,
after the radio stopped singing like a tree full of terrified frogs,
after night burst the dam of day and flooded the kitchen,
for a time the stoves glowed in darkness like the lighthouse in Fajardo,
like a cook's soul. Soul I say, even if the dead cannot tell us
about the bristles of God's beard because God has no face,
soul I say, to name the smoke-beings flung in constellations
across the night sky of this city and cities to come.
Alabanza I say, even if God has no face.

Alabanza. When the war began, from Manhattan and Kabul
two constellations of smoke rose and drifted to each other,
mingling in icy air, and one said with an Afghan tongue:
Teach me to dance. We have no music here.
And the other said with a Spanish tongue:
I will teach you. Music is all we have.

Glossary

alabanza: Praise; sometimes used in a religious sense; from 'alabar,' to celebrate with words.

arroz con pollo: Literally 'rice with chicken,' a common dish in Puerto Rico and Latin America.

barrio: Neighbourhood.

Barrio René Cisneros: Community constructed in Managua, Nicaragua, after the Sandinista Revolution (1978-1979) on land expropriated from the Somoza family that ruled the country for more than forty years; named for a combatant killed in that revolution.

botánica: Syncretic religious shop, specializing in spiritism, full of herbs, potions, statues, books, etc.

campesino: Peasant.

Clemente, Roberto: Hall of Fame baseball player from Puerto Rico who died in a 1972 plane crash delivering relief supplies to earthquake victims in Nicaragua.

compañero: Good friend; the word may also refer to a lover, or have connotations of political comradeship.

conga: Tall drum of West African origin.

guayabera: Long embroidered shirt, common in the Caribbean.

jardines del paraíso: The gardens of paradise.

huelga: Strike; a word often associated with César Chávez and the United Farm Workers.

maracas: Gourd rattles.

marimba: a xylophone, indigenous to Central America.

Miranda, Carmen: A very popular singer, dancer and movie actress from Brazil, known for her flamboyant costumes and headdresses, Miranda suffered a heart attack during a filming of *The Jimmy Durante Show* in 1955, then died at her home of a second heart attack several hours later.

La Migra: Refers to the U.S. Immigration and Customs Enforcement (ICE) agency.

oye: Literally, 'listen;' the equivalent of 'hey.'

salsa: Popular dance music which evolved in the Latino community of New York in the late 1960s.

ser o no ser: To be or not to be.

tabaqueros: Cigar makers.

Taíno: Original indigenous inhabitants of Puerto Rico, decimated by the Spanish.

taxista: cab driver.

tecato: Junkie.

mi vida: my life; sometimes serves as an expression of endearment, as here.

Vieques: Offshore island municipality of Puerto Rico, which was the site of live bombardment and war games by the U.S. Navy for decades, leading to high rates of cancer, unemployment and poverty.

Vocero, El: literally, an advocate or spokesperson; here, a sensationalist newspaper in Puerto Rico.

El Yunque: Rain forest in Puerto Rico, noted for its waterfalls.

Zapatista: Contemporary revolutionary movement based in Chiapas, México, and named for Emiliano Zapata, leader of the Mexican Revolution of 1910.

Acknowledgements

These poems originally appeared in the following collections by Martín Espada, and are used by permission of WW Norton & Company, Inc.:

City of Coughing and Dead Radiators (WW Norton, 1993): 'The Rifle in My Hands,' 'Transient Hotel Sky at the Hour of Sleep,' 'Who Burns for the Perfection of Paper,' 'City of Coughing and Dead Radiators,' 'Mi Vida: Wings of Fright,' 'The Broken Window of Rosa Ramos,' 'The Legal Aid Lawyer Has an Epiphany,' 'The Toolmaker Unemployed,' 'Prayer for Brother Burglar.'

Imagine the Angels of Bread (WW Norton, 1996): 'The Meaning of the Shovel,' 'Rednecks;' 'Do Not Put Dead Monkeys in the Freezer,' 'The Bouncer's Confession,' 'Thieves of Light,' 'Offerings to an Ulcerated God,' 'My Native Costume,' 'The Foreman's Wallet,' 'The Chair in the Dragon's Mouth,' 'Huelga.'

A Mayan Astronomer in Hell's Kitchen (WW Norton, 2000): 'The Death of Carmen Miranda,' 'The Janitor's Garden,' 'The Mexican Cabdriver's Poem for His Wife, Who Has Left Him,' 'For the Jim Crow Mexican Restaurant in Cambridge, Massachusetts, Where My Cousin Esteban was Forbidden to Wait Tables Because He Wears Dreadlocks.'

Alabanza: New and Selected Poems (WW Norton, 2003): 'Inheritance of Waterfalls and Sharks,' 'Latin Night at the Pawnshop,' 'Watch Me Swing,' 'The Saint Vincent de Paul Food Pantry Stomp,' 'Federico's Ghost,' 'The Florida Citrus Growers Association Responds to a Proposed Law Requiring Hand-Washing Facilities in the Fields,' 'Leo Blue's and the Tiger Rose,' 'Julio Signing His Name,' 'The Right Hand of a Mexican Farmworker in Somerset County, Maryland,' 'Jorge the Church Janitor Finally Quits.'

The Trouble Ball (WW Norton, 2011): 'My Heart Kicked Like a Mouse in a Paper Bag,' 'A Travelling Salesman in the Gardens of Paradise, 'The Poet's Son Watches His Father Leave for Another Gig.'